Hello!

This book belongs to:

What is Gratitude?

Gratitude is the feeling of thankfulness we have when someone gives us a present, helps, or encourages us with words.

Why keep a gratitude journal?

When you write in your journal, you have the chance to think about all of the things that you are thankful for.
This is how we practice gratitude!
We can be thankful for big things, small things and anything between.

My name is .....

And I am .....

I am ... years old!

My favorite:

 Color:

 Book:

 Food:

 Animal:

 Sport

 Animated Movie:

 Song:

 Place to go:

 Toy:

Date:

Today I am grateful for...

1) ....

2) ....

3) ....

4) ....

5) ....

I am ...

AWESOME!

SMART!

BLESSED!

This person brought me joy today ....

What was the best part about your day?
Draw or write about it...

I Feel...

| Happy | Worried | Sad | Angry | Bored |

Date:

Today I am grateful for...

1) ....

2) ....

3) ....

4) ....

5) ....

I am ...

AWESOME!

SMART!

BLESSED!

This person brought me joy today ....

What was the best part about your day?
Draw or write about it...

I Feel...

| Happy | Worried | Sad | Angry | Bored |

Date:

Today I am grateful for...

1) ....

2) ....

3) ....

4) ....

5) ....

This person brought me joy today ....

What was the best part about your day?
Draw or write about it...

I am ...

AWESOME!

SMART!

BLESSED!

I Feel...

Happy	Worried	Sad	Angry	Bored

Date:

Today I am grateful for...

1) ....

2) ....

3) ....

4) ....

5) ....

Hello!

I am ...

AWESOME!

SMART!

BLESSED!

This person brought me joy today ....

What was the best part about your day?
Draw or write about it...

I Feel...

Happy	Worried	Sad	Angry	Bored

Date:

Today I am grateful for...

1) ....

2) ....

3) ....

4) ....

5) ....

I am ...

AWESOME!

SMART!

BLESSED!

This person brought me joy today ....

What was the best part about your day?
Draw or write about it...

I Feel...

Happy	Worried	Sad	Angry	Bored

Date:

Today I am grateful for...

1) ....

2) ....

3) ....

4) ....

5) ....

I am ...

AWESOME!

SMART!

BLESSED!

This person brought me joy today ....

What was the best part about your day?
Draw or write about it...

I Feel...

Happy   Worried   Sad   Angry   Bored

Date:

Today I am grateful for...

1) ....

2) ....

3) ....

4) ....

5) ....

I am ...

AWESOME!

SMART!

BLESSED!

This person brought me joy today ....

What was the best part about your day?
Draw or write about it...

I Feel...

Happy	Worried	Sad	Angry	Bored

Date:

Today I am grateful for...

1) ....
2) ....
3) ....
4) ....
5) ....

I am ...

AWESOME!

SMART!

BLESSED!

Hello!

This person brought me joy today ....

What was the best part about your day?
Draw or write about it...

I Feel...

| Happy | Worried | Sad | Angry | Bored |

Date:

Today I am grateful for...

1) ....

2) ....

3) ....

4) ....

5) ....

I am ...

AWESOME!

SMART!

BLESSED!

This person brought me joy today ....

What was the best part about your day?
Draw or write about it...

I Feel...

Happy   Worried   Sad   Angry   Bored

Date:

Today I am grateful for...

I am ...

1) ....

AWESOME!

2) ....

SMART!

3) ....

BLESSED!

4) ....

5) ....

Hello!

This person brought me joy today ....

What was the best part about your day?
Draw or write about it...

I Feel...

Happy	Worried	Sad	Angry	Bored

Date:

Today I am grateful for...

1) ....

2) ....

3) ....

4) ....

5) ....

I am ...

AWESOME!

SMART!

BLESSED!

This person brought me joy today ....

What was the best part about your day?
Draw or write about it...

I Feel...

Happy	Worried	Sad	Angry	Bored

Date:

Today I am grateful for...

1) ....

2) ....

3) ....

4) ....

5) ....

I am ...

AWESOME!

SMART!

BLESSED!

This person brought me joy today ....

What was the best part about your day?
Draw or write about it...

I Feel...

| Happy | Worried | Sad | Angry | Bored |

Date:

Today I am grateful for...

1) ....
2) ....
3) ....
4) ....
5) ....

I am ...

AWESOME!

SMART!

BLESSED!

This person brought me joy today ....

What was the best part about your day?
Draw or write about it...

I Feel...

Happy	Worried	Sad	Angry	Bored

Date: ....

Today I am grateful for...

1) ....

2) ....

3) ....

4) ....

5) ....

I am ...

AWESOME!

SMART!

BLESSED!

This person brought me joy today ....

What was the best part about your day?
Draw or write about it...

I Feel...

Happy	Worried	Sad	Angry	Bored

Date:

Today I am grateful for...

1) ....

2) ....

3) ....

4) ....

5) ....

This person brought me joy today ....

What was the best part about your day?
Draw or write about it...

I am ...

AWESOME!

SMART!

BLESSED!

I Feel...

Happy	Worried	Sad	Angry	Bored

Date:

Today I am grateful for...

1) ....

2) ....

3) ....

4) ....

5) ....

I am ...

AWESOME!

SMART!

BLESSED!

This person brought me joy today ....

What was the best part about your day?
Draw or write about it...

I Feel...

Happy   Worried   Sad   Angry   Bored

Date:

Today I am grateful for...

1) ....

2) ....

3) ....

4) ....

5) ....

I am ...

AWESOME!

SMART!

BLESSED!

This person brought me joy today ....

What was the best part about your day?
Draw or write about it...

I Feel...

Happy   Worried   Sad   Angry   Bored

          Sad

Date:

Today I am grateful for...

1) ....

2) ....

3) ....

4) ....

5) ....

I am ...

AWESOME!

SMART!

BLESSED!

This person brought me joy today ....

What was the best part about your day?
Draw or write about it...

I Feel...

Happy	Worried	Sad	Angry	Bored

Date:

Today I am grateful for...

I) ....

I am ...

2) ....

AWESOME!

3) ....

SMART!

4) ....

BLESSED!

5) ....

This person brought me joy today ....!

What was the best part about your day?
Draw or write about it...

I Feel...

Happy	Worried	Sad	Angry	Bored

Date:

Today I am grateful for...

1) ....

2) ....

3) ....

4) ....

5) ....

This person brought me joy today ....

What was the best part about your day?
Draw or write about it...

I am ...

AWESOME!

SMART!

BLESSED!

I Feel...

Happy	Worried	Sad	Angry	Bored

Date:

Today I am grateful for...

I am ...

1) ....

AWESOME!

2) ....

SMART!

3) ....

BLESSED!

4) ....

5) ....

This person brought me joy today ....

What was the best part about your day?
Draw or write about it...

I Feel...

Happy   Worried   Sad   Angry   Bored

Date:

Today I am grateful for...

1) ....

2) ....

3) ....

4) ....

5) ....

I am ...

AWESOME!

SMART!

BLESSED!

This person brought me joy today ....

What was the best part about your day?
Draw or write about it...

I Feel...

Happy	Worried	Sad	Angry	Bored

Date:

Today I am grateful for...

1) ....

2) ....

3) ....

4) ....

5) ....

I am ...

AWESOME!

SMART!

BLESSED!

This person brought me joy today ....

What was the best part about your day?
Draw or write about it...

I Feel...

Happy	Worried	Sad	Angry	Bored

Date:

Today I am grateful for...

1) ....

2) ....

3) ....

4) ....

5) ....

I am ...

AWESOME!

SMART!

BLESSED!

Hello!

This person brought me joy today ....!....

What was the best part about your day?
Draw or write about it...

I Feel...

| Happy | Worried | Sad | Angry | Bored |

Date:

Today I am grateful for...

1) ....

2) ....

3) ....

4) ....

5) ....

I am ...

AWESOME!

SMART!

BLESSED!

This person brought me joy today ....

What was the best part about your day?
Draw or write about it...

I Feel...

Happy   Worried   Sad   Angry   Bored

Date:

Today I am grateful for...

1) ....

I am ...

2) ....

AWESOME!

3) ....

SMART!

4) ....

BLESSED!

5) ....

Hello!

This person brought me joy today ....

What was the best part about your day?
Draw or write about it...

I Feel...

Happy   Worried   Sad   Angry   Bored

Date:

Today I am grateful for...

1) ....
2) ....
3) ....
4) ....
5) ....

I am ...

AWESOME!

SMART!

BLESSED!

This person brought me joy today
....

What was the best part about your day?
Draw or write about it...

I Feel...

Happy	Worried	Sad	Angry	Bored

Date:

Today I am grateful for...

1) ....

2) ....

3) ....

4) ....

5) ....

I am ...

AWESOME!

SMART!

BLESSED!

This person brought me joy today ....

What was the best part about your day?
Draw or write about it...

I Feel...

Happy	Worried	Sad	Angry	Bored

Date:

Today I am grateful for...

I am ...

1) ....
2) ....
3) ....
4) ....
5) ....

AWESOME!

SMART!

BLESSED!

This person brought me joy today ....

What was the best part about your day?
Draw or write about it...

I Feel...

Happy   Worried   Sad   Angry   Bored

Date:

Today I am grateful for...

1) ....
2) ....
3) ....
4) ....
5) ....

This person brought me joy today ....

What was the best part about your day?
Draw or write about it...

I am ...

AWESOME!

SMART!

BLESSED!

I Feel...

Happy	Worried	Sad	Angry	Bored

Date:

Today I am grateful for...

1) ....

2) ....

3) ....

4) ....

5) ....

I am ...

AWESOME!

SMART!

BLESSED!

This person brought me joy today ....

What was the best part about your day?
Draw or write about it...

I Feel...

Happy	Worried	Sad	Angry	Bored

Date:

Today I am grateful for...

1) ....

2) ....

3) ....

4) ....

5) ....

I am ...

AWESOME!

SMART!

BLESSED!

This person brought me joy today ....

What was the best part about your day?
Draw or write about it...

I Feel...

Happy	Worried	Sad	Angry	Bored

Date:

Today I am grateful for...

1) ....

2) ....

3) ....

4) ....

5) ....

I am ...

AWESOME!

SMART!

BLESSED!

This person brought me joy today ....!...

What was the best part about your day?
Draw or write about it...

I Feel...

| Happy | Worried | Sad | Angry | Bored |

Date:

Today I am grateful for...

1) ....

2) ....

3) ....

4) ....

5) ....

I am ...

AWESOME!

SMART!

BLESSED!

Hello!

This person brought me joy today ....

What was the best part about your day?
Draw or write about it...

I Feel...

| Happy | Worried | Sad | Angry | Bored |

Date:

Today I am grateful for...

1) ....

2) ....

3) ....

4) ....

5) ....

I am ...

AWESOME!

SMART!

BLESSED!

This person brought me joy today ....

What was the best part about your day?
Draw or write about it...

I Feel...

Happy   Worried   Sad   Angry   Bored

Date:

Today I am grateful for...

I am ...

1) ....

AWESOME!

2) ....

SMART!

3) ....

BLESSED!

4) ....

5) ....

Hello!

This person brought me joy today ....

What was the best part about your day?
Draw or write about it...

I Feel...

Happy   Worried   Sad   Angry   Bored

Date:

Today I am grateful for...

1) ....

2) ....

3) ....

4) ....

5) ....

I am ...

AWESOME!

SMART!

BLESSED!

This person brought me joy today ....

What was the best part about your day?
Draw or write about it...

I Feel...

Happy   Worried   Sad   Angry   Bored

Date:

Today I am grateful for...

1) ....

I am ...

2) ....

AWESOME!

3) ....

SMART!

4) ....

BLESSED!

5) ....

This person brought me joy today ....

What was the best part about your day?
Draw or write about it...

I Feel...

Happy   Worried   Sad   Angry   Bored

Date:

Today I am grateful for...

I am ...

1) ....

AWESOME!

2) ....

SMART!

3) ....

BLESSED!

4) ....

5) ....

This person brought me joy today ....

What was the best part about your day?
Draw or write about it...

I Feel...

Happy   Worried   Sad   Angry   Bored

Date:

Today I am grateful for...

1) ....
2) ....
3) ....
4) ....
5) ....

I am ...

AWESOME!

SMART!

BLESSED!

This person brought me joy today ....

What was the best part about your day?
Draw or write about it...

I Feel...

Happy	Worried	Sad	Angry	Bored

Date:

Today I am grateful for...

1) ....
2) ....
3) ....
4) ....
5) ....

I am ...

AWESOME!

SMART!

BLESSED!

This person brought me joy today ....

What was the best part about your day?
Draw or write about it...

I Feel...

Happy	Worried	Sad	Angry	Bored

Date:

Today I am grateful for...

1) ....
2) ....
3) ....
4) ....
5) ....

I am ...

AWESOME!

SMART!

BLESSED!

This person brought me joy today ....

What was the best part about your day?
Draw or write about it...

I Feel...

Happy   Worried   Sad   Angry   Bored

Date:

Today I am grateful for...

I am ...

1) ....

AWESOME!

2) ....

3) ....

SMART!

4) ....

BLESSED!

5) ....

This person brought me joy today ....

What was the best part about your day?
Draw or write about it...

I Feel...

Happy   Worried   Sad   Angry   Bored

Date:

Today I am grateful for...

I) ....

I am ...

2) ....

AWESOME!

3) ....

SMART!

4) ....

BLESSED!

5) ....

Hello!

This person brought me joy today ....

What was the best part about your day?
Draw or write about it...

I Feel...

Happy	Worried	Sad	Angry	Bored

Date:

Today I am grateful for...

1) ....
2) ....
3) ....
4) ....
5) ....

I am ...

AWESOME!

SMART!

BLESSED!

Hello!

This person brought me joy today ....

What was the best part about your day?
Draw or write about it...

I Feel...

Happy   Worried   Sad   Angry   Bored

Date:

Today I am grateful for...

1) ....
2) ....
3) ....
4) ....
5) ....

I am ...

AWESOME!

SMART!

BLESSED!

Hello!

This person brought me joy today ....

What was the best part about your day?
Draw or write about it...

I Feel...

Happy   Worried   Sad   Angry   Bored

Date:

Today I am grateful for...

I) ....

2) ....

3) ....

4) ....

5) ....

I am ...

AWESOME!

SMART!

BLESSED!

This person brought me joy today ....!....

What was the best part about your day?
Draw or write about it...

I Feel...

Happy	Worried	Sad	Angry	Bored

Date:

Today I am grateful for...

1) ....

2) ....

3) ....

4) ....

5) ....

I am ...

AWESOME!

SMART!

BLESSED!

This person brought me joy today ....

What was the best part about your day?
Draw or write about it...

I Feel...

Happy	Worried	Sad	Angry	Bored

Date:

Today I am grateful for...

1) ....

2) ....

3) ....

4) ....

5) ....

I am ...

AWESOME!

SMART!

BLESSED!

This person brought me joy today ....

What was the best part about your day?
Draw or write about it...

I Feel...

Happy   Worried   Sad   Angry   Bored

Date:

Today I am grateful for...

1) ....

2) ....

3) ....

4) ....

5) ....

I am ...

AWESOME!

SMART!

BLESSED!

Hello!

This person brought me joy today ....

What was the best part about your day?
Draw or write about it...

I Feel...

Happy   Worried   Sad   Angry   Bored

Date:

Today I am grateful for...

1) ....

2) ....

3) ....

4) ....

5) ....

I am ...

AWESOME!

SMART!

BLESSED!

Hello!

This person brought me joy today ....

What was the best part about your day?
Draw or write about it...

I Feel...

| Happy | Worried | Sad | Angry | Bored |

Date:

Today I am grateful for...

1) ....

2) ....

3) ....

4) ....

5) ....

I am ...

AWESOME!

SMART!

BLESSED!

Hello!

This person brought me joy today ....

What was the best part about your day?
Draw or write about it...

I Feel...

Happy	Worried	Sad	Angry	Bored

Date:

Today I am grateful for...

1) ....

2) ....

3) ....

4) ....

5) ....

I am ...

AWESOME!

SMART!

BLESSED!

This person brought me joy today ....

What was the best part about your day?
Draw or write about it...

I Feel...

Happy   Worried   Sad   Angry   Bored

Date:

Today I am grateful for...

1) ....

2) ....

3) ....

4) ....

5) ....

I am ...

AWESOME!

SMART!

BLESSED!

This person brought me joy today ....

What was the best part about your day?
Draw or write about it...

I Feel...

Happy	Worried	Sad	Angry	Bored

Date:

Today I am grateful for...

1) ....

2) ....

3) ....

4) ....

5) ....

I am ...

AWESOME!

SMART!

BLESSED!

This person brought me joy today ....

What was the best part about your day?
Draw or write about it...

I Feel...

Happy	Worried	Sad	Angry	Bored

Date:

Today I am grateful for...

1) ....

2) ....

3) ....

4) ....

5) ....

I am ...

AWESOME!

SMART!

BLESSED!

This person brought me joy today ....

What was the best part about your day?
Draw or write about it...

I Feel...

Happy	Worried	Sad	Angry	Bored

Date:

Today I am grateful for...

I am ...

1) ....

AWESOME!

2) ....

3) ....

SMART!

4) ....

BLESSED!

5) ....

Hello!

This person brought me joy today ....

What was the best part about your day?
Draw or write about it...

I Feel...

| Happy | Worried | Sad | Angry | Bored |

Date:

Today I am grateful for...

1) ....

2) ....

3) ....

4) ....

5) ....

I am ...

AWESOME!

SMART!

BLESSED!

This person brought me joy today ....

What was the best part about your day?
Draw or write about it...

I Feel...

Happy	Worried	Sad	Angry	Bored

Date:

Today I am grateful for...

1) ....
2) ....
3) ....
4) ....
5) ....

I am ...

AWESOME!
SMART!
BLESSED!

This person brought me joy today ....

What was the best part about your day?
Draw or write about it...

I Feel...

Happy   Worried   Sad   Angry   Bored

Date:

Today I am grateful for...

1) ....

2) ....

3) ....

4) ....

5) ....

I am ...

AWESOME!

SMART!

BLESSED!

This person brought me joy today ....

What was the best part about your day?
Draw or write about it...

I Feel...

Happy	Worried	Sad	Angry	Bored

Date:

Today I am grateful for...

1) ....

I am ...

2) ....

AWESOME!

3) ....

SMART!

4) ....

BLESSED!

5) ....

This person brought me joy today ....

What was the best part about your day?
Draw or write about it...

I Feel...

Happy	Worried	Sad	Angry	Bored

Date:

Today I am grateful for...

1) ....

2) ....

3) ....

4) ....

5) ....

This person brought me joy today ....

I am ...

AWESOME!

SMART!

BLESSED!

Hello!

What was the best part about your day?
Draw or write about it...

I Feel...

Happy	Worried	Sad	Angry	Bored

Date:

Today I am grateful for...

1) ....

2) ....

3) ....

4) ....

5) ....

I am ...

AWESOME!

SMART!

BLESSED!

This person brought me joy today ....

What was the best part about your day?
Draw or write about it...

I Feel...

Happy	Worried	Sad	Angry	Bored

Date:

Today I am grateful for...

1) ....

2) ....

3) ....

4) ....

5) ....

I am ...

AWESOME!

SMART!

BLESSED!

This person brought me joy today ....

What was the best part about your day?
Draw or write about it...

I Feel...

| Happy | Worried | Sad | Angry | Bored |

Date:

Today I am grateful for...

1) ....

I am ...

2) ....

AWESOME!

3) ....

SMART!

4) ....

BLESSED!

5) ....

Hello!

This person brought me joy today ....

What was the best part about your day?
Draw or write about it...

I Feel...

Happy   Worried   Sad   Angry   Bored

Date:

Today I am grateful for...

1) ....

2) ....

3) ....

4) ....

5) ....

I am ...

AWESOME!

SMART!

BLESSED!

This person brought me joy today ....

What was the best part about your day?
Draw or write about it...

I Feel...

Happy	Worried	Sad	Angry	Bored

Date:

Today I am grateful for...

I am ...

1) ....

AWESOME!

2) ....

SMART!

3) ....

BLESSED!

4) ....

5) ....

Hello!

This person brought me joy today ....

What was the best part about your day?
Draw or write about it...

I Feel...

Happy　　　Worried　　　Sad　　　Angry　　　Bored

Date:

Today I am grateful for...

I am ...

1) ....

2) ....

AWESOME!

3) ....

SMART!

4) ....

BLESSED!

5) ....

This person brought me joy today ....

What was the best part about your day?
Draw or write about it...

I Feel...

Happy	Worried	Sad	Angry	Bored

Date:

Today I am grateful for...

I am ...

1) ....

AWESOME!

2) ....

SMART!

3) ....

BLESSED!

4) ....

5) ....

This person brought me joy today ....

What was the best part about your day?
Draw or write about it...

I Feel...

Happy   Worried   Sad   Angry   Bored

Date:

Today I am grateful for...

1) ....

2) ....

3) ....

4) ....

5) ....

I am ...

AWESOME!

SMART!

BLESSED!

Hello!

This person brought me joy today ....

What was the best part about your day?
Draw or write about it...

I Feel...

| Happy | Worried | Sad | Angry | Bored |

Date:

Today I am grateful for...

1) ....

2) ....

3) ....

4) ....

5) ....

This person brought me joy today ....

I am ...

AWESOME!

SMART!

BLESSED!

What was the best part about your day?
Draw or write about it...

I Feel...

Happy   Worried   Sad   Angry   Bored

Date:

Today I am grateful for...

1) ....
2) ....
3) ....
4) ....
5) ....

I am ...

AWESOME!

SMART!

BLESSED!

This person brought me joy today ....

What was the best part about your day?
Draw or write about it...

I Feel...

Happy	Worried	Sad	Angry	Bored

Date:

Today I am grateful for...

1) ....

2) ....

3) ....

4) ....

5) ....

I am ...

AWESOME!

SMART!

BLESSED!

This person brought me joy today ....

What was the best part about your day?
Draw or write about it...

I Feel...

Happy	Worried	Sad	Angry	Bored

Date:

Today I am grateful for...

I am ...

1) ....

2) ....

AWESOME!

3) ....

SMART!

4) ....

BLESSED!

5) ....

This person brought me joy today ....

What was the best part about your day?
Draw or write about it...

I Feel...

Happy	Worried	Sad	Angry	Bored

Date:

Today I am grateful for...

I am ...

1) ....
2) ....
3) ....
4) ....
5) ....

AWESOME!

SMART!

BLESSED!

This person brought me joy today ....

What was the best part about your day?
Draw or write about it...

I Feel...

Happy	Worried	Sad	Angry	Bored

Date: ....

Today I am grateful for...

1) ....

2) ....

3) ....

4) ....

5) ....

I am ...

AWESOME!

SMART!

BLESSED!

This person brought me joy today ....

What was the best part about your day?
Draw or write about it...

I Feel...

Happy	Worried	Sad	Angry	Bored

Date:

Today I am grateful for...

1) ....

2) ....

3) ....

4) ....

5) ....

I am ...

AWESOME!

SMART!

BLESSED!

This person brought me joy today ....

What was the best part about your day?
Draw or write about it...

I Feel...

Happy	Worried	Sad	Angry	Bored

Date:

Today I am grateful for...

1) ....
2) ....
3) ....
4) ....
5) ....

I am ...

AWESOME!

SMART!

BLESSED!

This person brought me joy today ....

What was the best part about your day?
Draw or write about it...

Hello!

I Feel...

| Happy | Worried | Sad | Angry | Bored |

Date:

Today I am grateful for...

1) ....

I am ...

2) ....

AWESOME!

3) ....

SMART!

4) ....

BLESSED!

5) ....

This person brought me joy today ....

What was the best part about your day?
Draw or write about it...

I Feel...

Happy   Worried   Sad   Angry   Bored

Date:

Today I am grateful for...

1) ....

2) ....

3) ....

4) ....

5) ....

I am ...

AWESOME!

SMART!

BLESSED!

This person brought me joy today ....!.....

What was the best part about your day?
Draw or write about it...

I Feel...

| Happy | Worried | Sad | Angry | Bored |

Date:

Today I am grateful for...

I am ...

1) ....

AWESOME!

2) ....

SMART!

3) ....

BLESSED!

4) ....

5) ....

This person brought me joy today ....

What was the best part about your day?
Draw or write about it...

I Feel...

| Happy | Worried | Sad | Angry | Bored |

Date:

Today I am grateful for...

1) ....

2) ....

3) ....

4) ....

5) ....

I am ...

AWESOME!

SMART!

BLESSED!

This person brought me joy today ....

What was the best part about your day?
Draw or write about it...

I Feel...

Happy   Worried   Sad   Angry   Bored

Date:

Today I am grateful for...

1) ....

2) ....

3) ....

4) ....

5) ....

I am ...

AWESOME!

SMART!

BLESSED!

This person brought me joy today ....

What was the best part about your day?
Draw or write about it...

I Feel...

Happy   Worried   Sad   Angry   Bored

Date:

Today I am grateful for...

1) ....

2) ....

3) ....

4) ....

5) ....

I am ...

AWESOME!

SMART!

BLESSED!

This person brought me joy today ....

What was the best part about your day?
Draw or write about it...

I Feel...

Happy	Worried	Sad	Angry	Bored

Date:

Today I am grateful for...

1) ....

2) ....

3) ....

4) ....

5) ....

I am ...

AWESOME!

SMART!

BLESSED!

This person brought me joy today ....

What was the best part about your day?
Draw or write about it...

I Feel...

Happy   Worried   Sad   Angry   Bored

Date:

Today I am grateful for...

1) ....

2) ....

3) ....

4) ....

5) ....

I am ...

AWESOME!

SMART!

BLESSED!

This person brought me joy today ....

What was the best part about your day?
Draw or write about it...

I Feel...

Happy   Worried   Sad   Angry   Bored

Date:

Today I am grateful for...

1) ....
2) ....
3) ....
4) ....
5) ....

I am ...

AWESOME!

SMART!

BLESSED!

This person brought me joy today ....

What was the best part about your day?
Draw or write about it...

I Feel...

Happy	Worried	Sad	Angry	Bored

Date:

Today I am grateful for...

1) ....

2) ....

3) ....

4) ....

5) ....

I am ...

AWESOME!

SMART!

BLESSED!

This person brought me joy today ....

What was the best part about your day?
Draw or write about it...

I Feel...

Happy	Worried	Sad	Angry	Bored

Date:

Today I am grateful for...

1) ....

2) ....

3) ....

4) ....

5) ....

This person brought me joy today ....

I am ...

AWESOME!

SMART!

BLESSED!

What was the best part about your day?
Draw or write about it...

I Feel...

| Happy | Worried | Sad | Angry | Bored |

Date: ....

Today I am grateful for...

1) ....
2) ....
3) ....
4) ....
5) ....

I am ...

AWESOME!

SMART!

BLESSED!

Hello!

This person brought me joy today ....

What was the best part about your day?
Draw or write about it...

I Feel...

Happy   Worried   Sad   Angry   Bored

Date:

Today I am grateful for...

1) ....

2) ....

3) ....

4) ....

5) ....

I am ...

AWESOME!

SMART!

BLESSED!

This person brought me joy today ....

What was the best part about your day?
Draw or write about it...

Hello!

I Feel...

Happy   Worried   Sad   Angry   Bored

Date:

Today I am grateful for...

1) ....

2) ....

I am ...

AWESOME!

3) ....

SMART!

4) ....

BLESSED!

5) ....

This person brought me joy today ....

What was the best part about your day?
Draw or write about it...

I Feel...

Happy   Worried   Sad   Angry   Bored

Date:

Today I am grateful for...

1) ....

2) ....

3) ....

4) ....

5) ....

I am ...

AWESOME!

SMART!

BLESSED!

This person brought me joy today ....

What was the best part about your day?
Draw or write about it...

Hello!

I Feel...

Happy   Worried   Sad   Angry   Bored

Date:

Today I am grateful for...

1) ....

2) ....

3) ....

4) ....

5) ....

This person brought me joy today ....

I am ...

AWESOME!

SMART!

BLESSED!

What was the best part about your day?
Draw or write about it...

I Feel...

Happy	Worried	Sad	Angry	Bored

Date:

Today I am grateful for...

1) ....
2) ....
3) ....
4) ....
5) ....

I am ...

AWESOME!

SMART!

BLESSED!

This person brought me joy today ....

What was the best part about your day?
Draw or write about it...

I Feel...

Happy   Worried   Sad   Angry   Bored

Date:

Today I am grateful for...

1) ....

2) ....

3) ....

4) ....

5) ....

This person brought me joy today ....

I am ...

AWESOME!

SMART!

BLESSED!

What was the best part about your day?
Draw or write about it...

I Feel...

Happy	Worried	Sad	Angry	Bored

Date: ....

Today I am grateful for...

1) ....
2) ....
3) ....
4) ....
5) ....

I am ...

AWESOME!

SMART!

BLESSED!

This person brought me joy today ....

What was the best part about your day?
Draw or write about it...

I Feel...

Happy   Worried Sad   Angry   Bored

Date:

Today I am grateful for...

1) ....

2) ....

3) ....

4) ....

5) ....

I am ...

AWESOME!

SMART!

BLESSED!

This person brought me joy today ....

What was the best part about your day?
Draw or write about it...

I Feel...

Happy	Worried	Sad	Angry	Bored

Date:

Today I am grateful for...

1) ....

2) ....

3) ....

4) ....

5) ....

I am ...

AWESOME!

SMART!

BLESSED!

Hello!

This person brought me joy today ....

What was the best part about your day?
Draw or write about it...

I Feel...

| Happy | Worried | Sad | Angry | Bored |

Date:

Today I am grateful for...

I am ...

1) ....

AWESOME!

2) ....

SMART!

3) ....

BLESSED!

4) ....

5) ....

Hello!

This person brought me joy today ....

What was the best part about your day?
Draw or write about it...

I Feel...

Happy   Worried   Sad   Angry   Bored

Date:

Today I am grateful for...

1) ....

2) ....

3) ....

4) ....

5) ....

I am ...

AWESOME!

SMART!

BLESSED!

This person brought me joy today ....

What was the best part about your day?
Draw or write about it...

I Feel...

Happy   Worried   Sad   Angry   Bored

Date:

Today I am grateful for...

1) ....

2) ....

3) ....

4) ....

5) ....

I am ...

AWESOME!

SMART!

BLESSED!

Hello!

This person brought me joy today ....

What was the best part about your day?
Draw or write about it...

I Feel...

Happy   Worried   Sad   Angry   Bored

Date:

Today I am grateful for...

1) ....

2) ....

3) ....

4) ....

5) ....

I am ...

AWESOME!

SMART!

BLESSED!

This person brought me joy today ....

What was the best part about your day?
Draw or write about it...

I Feel...

Happy   Worried   Sad   Angry   Bored

Date:

Today I am grateful for...

1) ....

2) ....

3) ....

4) ....

5) ....

I am ...

AWESOME!

SMART!

BLESSED!

This person brought me joy today ....

What was the best part about your day?
Draw or write about it...

I Feel...

Happy   Worried   Sad   Angry   Bored

Date:

Today I am grateful for...

1) ....

2) ....

3) ....

4) ....

5) ....

I am ...

AWESOME!

SMART!

BLESSED!

This person brought me joy today ....

What was the best part about your day?
Draw or write about it...

I Feel...

| Happy | Worried | Sad | Angry | Bored |

Date:

Today I am grateful for...

1) ....

2) ....

3) ....

4) ....

5) ....

I am ...

AWESOME!

SMART!

BLESSED!

This person brought me joy today ....

What was the best part about your day?
Draw or write about it...

I Feel...

| Happy | Worried | Sad | Angry | Bored |

Date:

Today I am grateful for...

1) ....

2) ....

3) ....

4) ....

5) ....

I am ...

AWESOME!

SMART!

BLESSED!

This person brought me joy today ....

What was the best part about your day?
Draw or write about it...

I Feel...

| Happy | Worried | Sad | Angry | Bored |

Made in United States
North Haven, CT
15 January 2022

14846493R00063